something close to god

something close to god

Erika Del Carmen Ruiz

Querencia Press - Chicago Illinois

QUERENCIA PRESS

ISBN 978 1 959118 78 7

www.querenciapress.com

First Published in 2024

Querencia Press, LLC
Chicago IL

Printed & Bound in the United States of America

for my mother,
who watches over me.

for Maria, Eva, Rocio, and Cristina
who love me unconditionally.

for my friends, who hold me
when i grieve and gift me new life.

“i scream into my own hands
and think
‘this is the portal to heaven’”

—from *i'm alive. it hurts. i love it.*
by Joshua Jennifer Espinoza—

CONTENTS

the poor in spirit

heart wounds

in the crowded backyard of the house
where i was an ephemeral being,
a nervous discomfort settled between us.

the late april air was thick with the clingy despair
of my dejected spirit, the uncomfortable emotion engulfing
the night's atmosphere as if it were a foretelling testament
of all the ways we would fall apart.

that night, i was nothing but a ball of anxiety
idealizing wishes that wouldn't come. and
he was a flighty ghost manifesting projections
of my unfulfilled longings.

in front of me—green canvas jacket and lips pursed
between flushed cheeks, a quiet yet restless disposition
of a man unfurling in the presence of panicked vulnerability.

us—two heart wounds beating with evasive movements,
sheepish avoidance, and misplaced self-worth.
even while nervously sat next to him—body carefully angled
on the white bench, there was the detectable distance.

all i could do was intently watch him through his protective
barrier. capture the memory as a sacred snapshot
that only momentarily existed.

with my heart smeared onto me, i acted as if
i hadn't spent the previous night crying.
as if i wasn't high on the feeling of stepping
into the dangers of emotional sensitivity.

my hands curled into themselves; the craving
for intimacy i struggled to give was a germinating
seed that presented my insecurities back to me.

through him, i saw only myself
and he was an image of everything
i thought i couldn't be.

today i feel like i'm dying and i'm trying not to be dramatic about it

on the way home,
i almost ran myself over with a bus

then texted three people about how it feels
like i'm ripping myself out of my chest.

but it's probably just stress. or the fact
that i've realized nothing i feel is real.

if you also came to this conclusion today,
you too would cry, and we could sit

together to wallow
in our pity.

this would heal us i think,
or at least keep us going.

i want to keep going.
but i don't know where that is.

i turned to my past self
in hopes that she'd have an answer

but she blankly stared
and i watched as old pain twisted her face

into something that looked like a frown
but was felt much deeper.

it's painful to watch
her despondency.

i’m ashamed she exists.
i hate that i am her.

my gender seeks out god

before i was taught to be a girl, i was first
a wailing child baptized in holy water.

curly haired, brown, and draped in white,
this is how my mother gifted me her religion.
she taught me to cradle it as an extension of who i was.

i learned that my body was a vessel for prayer.
i muttered psalms through a childhood
where catholicism was the only place i felt holy.

under god, the fragile fat kid feels a sense of purpose.
so i knelt, asked to be freed of sin, and pretended
that fatness didn't feel like a forced penance.

as if i owed everyone feminine thinness,
a dainty and quiet duty, a girlhood
that could fit neatly into a small display box.

i tried to comply, couldn't detach myself
from the pieces of me that grew too big
and bulged out of constraining things not meant to hold me.

at the same age that i first understood i was fat,
i first experienced (and repressed) gender dissociative panic
while fervently clinging to the god who loved me despite it.

i became a flagellant believer. found self-worth
in everything outside me, couldn't be a perfect girl
but i could be a devoted follower to a god
who treated my flaws with a softness that i couldn't.

but queerness demanded attention
and the hostile history of catholicism stole god from me,
i was alone in a flawed body that believed
the pain it experienced was spiritual payment.

i didn't know this was an act of martyrdom,
that, from it, i would emerge a fat queer saint
who understands the depth of god.

who transcends a human body,
comes back to themself,
and gives divine forgiveness.

anxiety attack ritual

at night, in a blanket of darkness,
when the one a.m. shadows transform
into a reminder of my self-pity,
i claw off my skin.

chunks of old memories get trapped
under my nails, their desperation
leaves lasting stains on my fingers
and my hands become a road map
of all the things i've ever lost.

i'm always saying goodbye to something.
throughout the years, it has evolved into a habitual ache.
a dull and common twinge. a constant, throbbing alarm,
letting me know that the world isn't mine,

that i don't belong anywhere. haha.
isn't it funny being trapped
in a prison of my own making?
there's so much that never made it past want.

god and i are in a complicated relationship

it's toxic and on-and-off again.
i'm always the one who tries to break it off
but then comes crawling back.

the disregarded prayers of my swollen tongue
dissolve in the distance between here and heaven.
where does my begging go?

an empty tension sits in the air between us.
god leaves me hanging without an answer,
ghosts, and then expects me to still love him.

i can't stand his silence. in my head,
my mother's voice calls. she says to leave
absent men but to devote myself to an absent god.

this is a war within me. i respond by becoming
a liminal terrain, the uncomfortable
wobble of an unsteady ground.

you'd think that years of practicing this balance
would prepare me for anxiety. that i'd learn grace
or, at least, how to fake my way through panic.

that i wouldn't be crying in frantic search
for the love i was promised. for the love that never came.

i don't want to accuse my mother of lying.
i don't want to yell at her grave or blame her
for the ways abandonment enveloped me.

how was she to know that god treated us differently?
that all my prayers got lost inside a void
but that some of them came ricocheting back

in the sound of my own voice. all i could do
was give into the raw and exposed treble.
oh my god, do you know how much that hurt?

somewhere between birth and breathing

this is where i learned to apologize.
my mouth, a splinter of a broken record,
a dial tuned to the same redemptive station
where the music is a piteous song lost in white static.

my brown body is an incoherent noise
colored like my father's loud rancheras.
a sound that can't undo. that makes it impossible
to gracefully drown in dramatics without it coming out
in gaudy sobs that mimic accordion sensitivity.

i'm an emo song with loud trumpets. a whiny cry
too eager for attention. an awful plastered melody
of all that has hurt me displayed
through screaming that is convinced it is art.

let me parade my pain for you. please,
i'm begging. pick at it as if it's something
that can be molded towards beauty.
convince me i'm valuable. that there is
more to this than depression dragging me
through the thickness of displaced diasporic trauma.

my gender is working class

in the two-story duplex, with the yard
where the dead dogs were buried, we lived
cramped in the half-finished house.

the hoarded piles of "just in case" objects.
the rundown cars collecting dust and debris in the driveway.
the stray cats we fed old scraps.

i was a child made of plump tears
and skinned knees, fifth daughter
watching the world with candid innocence.
a last addition to the things
my parents accumulated for years.

i was born into these habits,
the bed where i slept lumped with my sisters.
the converted garage turned room
overflowing with belongings we didn't use.
everything that overcompensated for the scarcity.

the stacked boxes full of knickknacks. the heap of overgrown
clothes, sat limp on the old couch. the gathered trinkets
lined up on the bulky shelf. the items we lost

when the house was foreclosed,
when they wouldn't let us back in.
when they locked it and took it from us for good.

god doesn't exist

in the empty performance that disguises unspoken sin.
in the sobbing lost through anxious translation. like secrets well-guarded.
like queerness slithering where conformity refuses to sit.

*

until the brittle bite of the eucharist sticks to my tongue.
until my mother's prayers become a dense swallowing.

until my mouth, half open, refuses to let out loud sobs
and the inkling that should've destroyed me,
instead, becomes a resounding psalm.

*

mother, i know how this goes:

silence, worn thin at the seams
of a devoted catholicism.
your prayers, a hum of idolatry.
and the image of god sits on the living room wall,

european jesus, his white hands signaling
in a welcoming blessing i can no longer follow.
if he had stayed brown, his image presented through history,
clay skin—half a mirror of me—

the isolation that accompanied would've been easier to swallow
and the disarray of emotions a gentler sting.

*

but loneliness tried to chew me. chomp me down
with its gritting teeth and turn my skin into nothing.

what was i supposed to do?
yell at the emptiness caught in my throat?
become her daughter how she wanted me to?
climb out of my body?

beg to an unflawed god?

a white god?
a male god?
a false god?

i can't follow a god like that.
how do i tell my mother?

becoming

i sat alone in my room and swallowed the stars
until transformation begged for release.
the burning sensation rested in the pit of my stomach,
wanted to be a guiding light into oblivion.

it called for carefree deliverance
but i was accustomed
to the eerie silence of darkness
that enveloped me in fragile dreams.

how did this happen?

there was nothing but a pitch black sea,
nothing but untamed universe pouring out from me
and filling the empty sky in erratic tragedy.

i was so ashamed of the outpour.

how i couldn't contain it.
how i had to surrender.
how it took control and guided me
wherever it decided to.

fat girl has a complicated relationship with pleasure

fat girl has a complicated relationship with pleasure.
can't distinguish between desire and what she deserves.
doesn't touch herself intimately, lets hands gather cobwebs
and be constant reminders of a failed self-compassion.

fat girl believes affection is something that's fleeting
or comes with a catch. traps her in a cycle
of people who merely want her as secret. who don't want
to admit she draws them in like a flame attracts moths.

fat girl can't tell the difference between trauma and love.
they both make hands shake, the heart thud.
everything about them translates as an anxious needy mess
calling out for attention and none of it ever feels like enough.

nightly ritual

take off your skin. let it sit in a heap
next to the bed where the cat can curl up to it.

it is okay if this is the only way you let yourself
be gently touched. the cat knows no better,

is conditioned to seek out soft warmth
and your skin is a perfect bedding.

fall asleep in bare organs. like this, the exhaustion
that comes with living shouldn't attack you until morning.

the next day, when you pick up your skin to put it back on,
wash out the stains from yesterday. iron out the creases.

slink into it as if you haven't before
and call it a new day.

how to disappoint your mother without her knowing

tell her you love her, say it in ways that make the words coming out of your mouth feel like styrofoam pressed against your teeth. it's squeak travels to your spine in a chilly recollection of lies. repeat the hymns she taught you, say them backwards, under your breath where blasphemy clicks on your tongue and clings to your neck.

*

write her name in the crevice of your breasts, underneath your eyelids, anywhere vulnerability might seep in. let it burn itself on your skin. welcome the scars. treat them with homemade remedies made from plastered anxiety and the refusal of god. use poetry to patch up the wounds. let them fester. become part of your body.

*

when you are tempted to show her your pain, cut off your tongue. hide it inside of a jar on bookshelves lined with dangerous specimens that double as weapons. tell her you love her. let the words sink in your stomach and mix in with the acid until their only option is to develop the symptoms of caring too much.

bargaining the trauma bond

what if i had made myself smaller/ had amputated
the weight of emotional baggage i carried/ had silenced
the sound of my crying/ had restrained my reactions
and bottled them up as a numb explosion within me/ imagine
being the same brand of coward/ like the man who is merely
a deceptive delusion of the charade he tries to be/ i admit/
i was a dumb animal drawn in by his aggressive mimicry/ the lies
by omission that only relayed/ what he could use to manipulate
with/ i was a fool dancing for him in the perceived safety
of his promises/ the wandering bear caught in a trap/ how fitting
that/ at the end/ i still stayed calm/ still entertained his illusion/
despite my anxiety/ still quietly let him discard me like trash.

gerard way gave birth to me

middle school, i was a vampire
pretending to be a girl. the fictional
books i habitually devoured as bible,

the carefully dramatized words
reminding me that i could someday
be an otherworldly being.

i emerged in 2005 as graceless child
trying to find an identity amidst the ruins.
i was ten-years-old and already self-conscious
of the space i reluctantly took up.

through the summer, when i slept achingly
on the hardwood floor with the inflatable bed,
my teenage sisters would enact an ongoing ritual:

press play on the vhs tape
with the recorded mtv videos.
i'd drift into dreams with pop punk songs
blaring as modern-day hymns.

every day, the sound of third-wave emo
welcomed me into tweenhood.
i memorized the order of songs
as they held me through the transition

where i started to embody full truth.
in the gawky blundering of becoming,
i began to decipher the sound of my voice
speaking to me from my throat.

the relentless emotional release
that came out uncomfortably
in finicky growing pains
i was embarrassed to experience.

daily, the man on the tv taught me
about catharsis. his vocals
resonating loudly in the hot night.

there was a sacredness about the sound of a man
who was intimately acquainted with heartache.
who could sing with lungs full of screams,
crying and purging with grace.

the sound of my life as it scraped blood
from the concrete. the fantasies
of freeing myself from the constraints.

there was an element to it
that almost felt like dying,
a romanticized self-demolition
disguised as artistic pursuit.

i watched him, the calculated dramatics
conveying full sorrow. teaching me
about unapologetic grief and the way
that it beats under the rib cage.

what holy release,
i absorbed the power vicariously.

the music carried me

—for Gem

in a small bedroom of the house
where i was transient,
i lived enveloped in claustrophobic loneliness.
the four walls were a protective cocoon
and, in them, i existed naked and bare
in the blissful comfort of despondent dreams.

in this womb, i was a fetus emerging
as the forsaken offspring of god,
a fledgling finding nourishment in ritualistic sobbing.

sometimes, this meant relinquishing,
being a body that was barely holding on,
a lump curled under blankets
with arms swollen and red
from relentless anxious scratching.

on the days when i failed to swallow myself,
i balanced my petulance in the space between
silence and song—the sound acting like a buffer
to soften the impact of self-deprecating falling apart.

it was ephemeral salvation: vinyl record scratching
wobbly on the portable crosley, a plastic needle that skipped
every time on the same beat, and the soft tremor of a voice,
halfway across the world, calling to me as a conjuring.

in this stillness, i was coming undone. unlearning allegiance
to scars that falsely promised me heaven.
the melodies, mimicking the sound in my bones,
unknowingly guided me forward

until the relentless longing for freedom
finally simmered into a muted memory
of things i have survived.

meeting the virgin mary on top of a hill overlooking san bernardino

"'Juan Diego' the Virgin said:
'This is the hill I've chosen
for my altar to be built'"
—translated from La Guadalupana

i was restless baby queer: a dissociated lump of pessimism
dripping sadness from my filthy pores, lost child
smoking herb as a form of self-compassion.

stupidly, i romanticized the dullness. every day, the struggle
of dragging myself clumsily against the worn out carpet, the dim
glare of the afternoon sun bleeding in through the window,
the weight on my chest as i roused from anxious sleep. monotony.

i was twenty-two and alive in ways that clamored.
eagerly, i awaited some kind of rebirth but everything
was masked in transient passing.

several days a week, i was forced out of bed by friends
who softly cared for me. who didn't ask questions.
who let me sit silently in the back of the moving car
as we hotboxed through the winding roads.

we were a spatter of young adult depression
struggling to help each other from caving in.
the car was a sanctuary. the windows,
a boundary that kept us from collapsing.

a spontaneous ritual—sometimes
it was the singular daily miracle that kept me
somewhat grounded. it laid a foundation
on which i could step out and squint at the moving world.

routinely, we'd end up in front of the house
of the man who sometimes yelled at us.
the valley expanded below, the lights
twinkling through the concentrated smog.

it was a makeshift heaven i couldn't find anywhere else.
where apparitions came and made me
accept the tenderness of the current moment.

a fleeting glimmer of the ethereal
where i could finally relax.
in the released outbreath,
the transfiguration started occurring.

in these moments of peace and levity
that contrasted against the discomfort,
i rebuilt myself as human church standing
solid on sacred ground. the burning flower
was an offering, the smoke a blessed incense,
and the outstretch of crowded city
was a congregation witnessing my chosen arrival.

i'm scared to ask my father if he feels free

i know he'll say yes. that we'll bond
over this and my mother's death
will be a cord cut that led us to freedom.

i hate to admit i was waiting for her to die
so i could fly without guilt attached to me.
that she passed away with us fighting
about my constant absence from church.

on sunday evenings, when she spent
her last months praising god
with my sisters in the quaint parish,
i spent those nights crying alone at home;
an unintentional mockery of her ceremonial routine.

sometimes, from my room, i could hear my father's voice
resonating loudly through the vacant house. doors closed,
the second-story floor between us, an alienating estrangement.

both of us and the constant avoidance
of my mother's expectations.
we craved release from the defeat.

for months, every sunday passed like this.
i couldn't bring myself to slide into a pew
and split my chest open. i was a sermon
on contrition, a confession that couldn't
blurt it out to anybody but the silence.

i don't know when my father learned
the act of numbness. his slow detachment
from church was a perfected artform.

the disenchantment in my mother's voice.
the separation between them that slowly grew wider
until they were strangers cohabiting the same room.

i watched my father live hidden behind a shadow.
imitated his disguise by camouflaging my ache
as an act of rebellion. chose the safest form
of disappointment. couldn't claim it
as self-imposed penance for queerness,

couldn't tell her i felt undeserving.
that i would break down in the middle of mass,
run out crying. that i couldn't go back.
pretended i stopped going because i didn't want to.

those who mourn

processing grief

the wood paneled floor of the kitchen
holds me and the tremors of my bawling.

i'm a human puddle of overthinking,
collapsed sad girl trapped in the drama
of my own trauma-filled story.

it's 2 p.m. and the empty house
is a chamber for the crying
my body can no longer withhold.

i'm embarrassed of my sobbing—
how the sound comes out
as a wretched ball of grating emotion.

in the background, ian curtis sings
the perfected art of gracefully collapsing.

i act like that's also what i'm doing,
it's the only way to suppress
my internalized shame from surfacing.

i lay on the dirty kitchen floor, my head resting
on a small cluster of gathered crumbs.
the half-washed dishes wait idly in the nearby sink.

each day passes like this:

> i try to act alive by hyperfocusing
> on a task that should be easy to overcome.
> but my emotions are an ongoing flood.
>
> out of hopelessness, i succumb to the desperate feeling.
> i momentarily let go of the false pretense
> that i have the capacity to be anything
> but an aching monument to misery.

the dirty dishes take hours to wash,
the floor rarely gets swept,
and i crumble into the wailing.

death as a commodity under capitalism

before my mother was routinely a hospital patient,
she used to sell catholic cemetery plots
as if they were samples from AVON.

she'd go house to house, convincing strangers
that death was imminent, that it was
a looming disaster of fleeting mortality

and the only way to somewhat alleviate
the oncoming pain was to be prepared.
    i.e. to shill out their money, i.e. to own
    the clumped dirt where their dead
    body would someday undisturbingly rot.

there is a calculated art of exploitation
to the method of selling cemetery plots effectively.
the customer has to be manipulated with fear.

there are entire trainings dedicated to this practice,
stories of unprepared families
and their consequences tucked under the tongue.

in between laminated flow charts and bible verses
of returning to the earth as dust, the customer
has to be convinced that this is the only viable option.

that this is the best way to quell the panic that comes with dying.
that salvation means nothing if grieving family
is left last-minute scrambling.

smiling, my mother would sell death
with the self-awareness
that soon she too might also die.

that under a society prioritizing money,
it is an unfortunate act of compassion
to softly exploit that anxiety.

to offer a preemptive solution.
to know that human existence is fleeting
and to use that knowledge as a way
to keep her family alive.

people who say i'm too fat also blamed my mother for her diabetes

yes, it killed her.
i've had this discussion before.

i know she neglected seeing a doctor for years,
drank whole liters of soda, ate too much bread,
and left this world after years of being hooked
to a machine that cleaned out her blood
because her kidneys couldn't function anymore.

this is an old story.

one that's brought up
to try and scare me
into making my body get thinner.

before my mother's diabetes made her lose
half her weight, she was a corpulent earth.
colossal flesh taking up space, a mouth
lost in the thickness, a ravenous
immigrant body suffering in a hostile country.

here, she slowly eroded.
spent too long doubling her back as a fortress
protecting five daughters from impact.

if this makes her responsible for her death,
then am i also at fault for consuming the ways
i was taught to hate my own flesh?

like my mother, my fat sits on bones
brittle from years of stewing disaster. it sags
in heavy bags of brown skin stretched to fit
the solid emotions i swallow.

sometimes, to balance the weight,
i let the density eat at itself.

is this how my life ends? will i someday
be nothing more than reflection of pain
once emitting from a fat person now gone?

now null? now reduced to mere warning
passed down as a hostile threat?

the deteriorating house

this house is a monument dedicated to the girl i'm shedding.
i have no parting gift to give her but a whimper of lament
for the anticipated futures that won't be.

in the hushed ambience of the consecrated back porch,
i've spent so long being a barely-living corpse
that acts on defensive impulse.
meat that wails as an inborn safeguard response.

today, instead, i choose the silence. with my hands,
i aimlessly pick at scabs on my legs that are slow to heal.
my nails dig into the brittle scars, blood pools and slowly trickles out,
and the last five years accidentally dribble onto my fingers.

in this moment, i placidly sit and stare at the mountains.
the outline of faraway pine trees contrast against the evening sky.
together, we are a symphony of broken dreams,
kin reflecting infinite existence back at each other.

i know no deeper devotion than the one that comes
in the form of defeat. in this vulnerable position,
i unveil the sorrow that sits underneath, the one i've learned

to avoid, push down, swallow. i let the ache surface,
it gurgles in the warm air. i softly breathe out and everything tumbles.

i contemplated suicide and my grandmother appeared in a dream

my teeth were rotting as i swallowed my spit,
i was drunk, and everything resembled a weapon.

it's not that i wanted to die

but my breathing called out fleetingly to the moon
and enticed the cord that sat right by my hand.

maybe that's why i thought about grabbing it.

the next morning, hungover,
i sat on the couch and couldn't stop feeling

like a cankering sore stuck to the earth. i still lived

in the house where my grandmother choked.
it happened so quickly, and she was so frail

the bread got stuck in her throat.

if i'd known it would kill her,
i wouldn't have given her dinner,

but maybe i'm destined to be a grim reaper
and suffocatingly carry demise wrapped around my neck.

i recognized death in her face when it came. had sat beside it all day
during the months that she lay in the hospital bed:

both of us strangled by anxious depression,
i thought we'd be smothered by it.
that it would choke us until we were nothing.

there were so many times it almost did happen.
when we couldn't stop crying, our breath wouldn't stop coming.

it's not that we wanted to die

but trauma cuts off all oxygen, replaces it
with internal strife. how am i supposed to explain
what it was like to watch her live at the cusp of possibly dying?

to have a mouth that is a sepulcher for wounds?
how she felt it too and our empathetic hearts were
consumed?

two nights after i almost choked myself to sleep,
she came to me in my dreams: radiant, alive, and existing.

i felt compelled to apologize to the sun
who can no longer bathe her each morning,
who would miss me if i inhaled sorrow too deeply
and stopped breathing.

but i'm alive. i'm not leaving.
it is okay to be stuck to the earth.

every day i cycle through the motions of grief
and things just keep happening that prolong it

please stop. i'm so tired
of carrying this on my shoulders.

i want the feeling to dissipate,
let me breathe for once. remind me

i am more than this sadness. that i can
get out of bed, be a person, or at least

try to exist half-hollowed, sideways,
an imitation of what i was trying to be.

yesterday, i spent all day picking
at the agony stuck to my bones

and i burned off the excess,
lit it on fire and laughed as i started to disappear.

it made me feel so alive.
i was so radiant, everything was perfect.

watching my mother break down in grief

in the hospital room
where my dead grandmother lay,

i watch my mother transform into five-year-old child
lost in the midst of adulthood. her sobs come out

as a plea, her hands cupping
the body's cold cheeks.

she cries with a force full of desperation,
the hopeless sound of a woman begging.

in the crack of her voice, i can hear the years
she spent being an extension of her mother's care.

born to only brothers,
she was a daughter who inherited a burden

of labor expected without recognition.
the act of holding the earth.

of being the lifeforce sustaining
a family of cataclysmic men

shaped like dull weapons.
their absence until my grandmother's death.

my mother becoming
her mother's keeper:

a bond shaped beyond blood,
of women who kept each other alive.

who survived while carrying
the heavy weight with them.

purgatory

i know this feeling. i met it once
before, in the emptiness
that followed my mother's death.

the hopelessness of it forces
abject surrender, self buckling
under the weight of all that's stayed unsaid.

in this limbo in hell, i'm a pendulum
hanging in concentrated loss.
i atone for the sins i committed against myself.

here, i say goodbye to everything that's left me behind,
that's chosen to prioritize comfortable dysfunction over me.
i yell. i break down. i let it all out.

some farewells are said as silent heaviness,
the bargaining we no longer touch. the arguing
we let simmer. the release that hurts too much
and dangles as gaslit disappointment.

who am i now? outside of the homes
i tried to make that decided
they'd no longer hold me?

who am i but a newborn suckling
on the tit of unbridled resurrection,
a tiny and fragile thing relearning
dexterity in the wind.

beneath the layers, where i sit
naked and crouched into myself,
i find a frightened animal accustomed
to feeling cornered with anxiety.

with it, all that's left of me collapses.

my mother is dead

this is my most central truth now.

everything about me is tethered to it,
will always be tethered to it:

my mother is dead
and she will be dead forever.

i'll know no other life,
i'll feel no other wholeness.

i'm alone, i'm orphaned.
with softness, i tend to this grief.

we reluctantly inhabit the same body:
my eyes are its eyes, its feelings are my feelings,

we exist as one entity
enmeshed with itself.

there is no difference between us
now. i breathe, it breathes.

to fully see me is to pay witness
to this hollow within me.

to deem it as holy. to be present
as i hold myself through it.

helping to mother the dying

i was seventeen when every day blurred
into the same traumatic memory
that would continue to plague me years later.
after the hospitals, after the lawyers,
after her spirit had made its way home.

i molded my identity through it, cradling her frail body.
what i know of motherhood, i learned through helping
my grandmother survive a history that never saved her.
the routine diaper changes, the feedings,
the late nights struggling while she screamed
for a dead mother who never came to comfort her.

sometimes, the sound of our crying blended
perfectly into each other like a song
lost in its own longing. through my distress,
i watched the old woman suffer and regress
into a child who had lost all autonomy,
who had no other option but to live barely coherent.

she didn't know who i was. routinely, i cleaned out
her intimacy but it was an act that had lost all meaning.
the dementia made her forget. often she'd yell
that it was a violation to her body. and wasn't it?
to keep her alive when she didn't want to be,
when she refused to eat and wanted to decay
into a pile of sacred bones that had known a life
rich with decisions she would make on her own.

it all happened so suddenly: the cardiac arrest,
the leg amputation, her brain rewiring itself to protect her
from the bodily trauma that made her lose full control.
nobody knew how to maneuver through it gracefully,
we fumbled while struggling to keep her afloat.

i was a child, barely seventeen,
caregiving for a woman who had given birth
to endless children who were now grown men.
where were they? it was only the women: my sisters,
my mother who was also sick, also dying.
we were tending, cleaning, looking after her.

with them, i learned to carry trauma twice my size
better than any man ever could. from within me,
i pulled out a strength they would never be able to name.
i learned to protect my grandmother. to live vicariously
for her, if i had to. to simultaneously build my whole life through it.

my mother and i sustain a relationship post-mortem

it's june and i'm falling apart with mourning.
under the full moon, all i experience is your absence.
the loss that permeates the quiet house where i float in lonely grief.

i feel your spirit everywhere, in the chasms
you left behind. but my hands only grasp thin air.

tonight, i cry sitting cross legged on the dirty cement,
back resting against my sister's gray car.
something about this feels sacred:

i uncover queer truth, let it air out in the tepid summer night.
suddenly i can't hide. i'm so aware that you see me
uncovered, that i ooze with the pain i've concealed.

mother, do you witness me?
am i holy enough in my truth?
do i also make it to heaven,
even with queerness?

i'm sorry i hid it. i didn't know how to live
in the dichotomy that pulled us apart.

do you remember the day we sat together,
intensely, in the dark room? it was 2015,
you were thin with sickness, and i was on fire.

my head was resting on your fragile thighs, your hands
gently but worryingly caressing my misery like a mother
protecting her child in the only way she knows how.

i couldn't stop crying, you heard me but couldn't listen.
a loud silence between us that permeated with years
of catholic indoctrination, of heterosexual compulsion.
i was trying to come out. i wanted to display true self
like broken sorrow,

let you cradle me in the raw uncovering of who i was.
was i expecting too much? mother, in heaven
where you have access to everything, are you watching
my pain unfurl throughout the years you didn't know about?

do you see my ache now?
mother, please tell me i'm worthy.

i'm always prepared to die

each morning, i asses what it means to exist
stuck to the earth in a meat sack

that will someday be nothing
more than a corpse in the dirt.

on most days, i run away
from the parts of me

that resemble broken blood vessels
ruptured on discolored skin.

drag me out of here,   please.
                                    it hurts

too much to let it be.
maybe, if i rip myself out,

the feelings will stop, won't hit.
won't eat at my guts

or be overwhelming agony. wow,
look at me live as if i'm not perishable.

as if i shouldn't be scared of the insignificance
that comes with tomorrow. and the next day.

or the years i thought i wouldn't survive to see.
when i thought this life was a myth

fed to me as a bribe to retain me in suffering.
these old habits cling to my chest,

a raspy outbreath confused as a longing cry
telling a story in which i want to kill myself.

is this the reality of where i sit? my hands,
two resting weapons attached to me.

if so, why am i still here? it is so easy
to find death in everything.

letting go

in this room,
i hold a funeral.

i am the body
the cleric
the pallbearer
the mourner.

the scattered piles on the floor
act like makeshift bereavement flowers,
small pops of color against the dark hardwood.

the temporary twin sized mattress
i inhabit is my unplanned coffin.
i lay here, subdued in the silence.

friend, grieve with me. i will release
this outdated life, i promise. just help me
mumble the nine days of prayer

so that i can arrive renewed
and forgiven wherever heaven is.
so that i can be baptized again
and be gifted new life.

twenty-five days after my mother's death

i haven't drowned the mop in bleach
how she told me to do
on the evening she left to the hospital
and never came back.

it's sitting, leaning against
the laundry room wall,
smelling of dirt and decay.

the stench demands my attention
but i refuse to give in even as it pulls
at the airways leading up to my nostrils.

how long can i pretend it doesn't exist?
that the echoes from past versions of me
don't rebound off my skin in dingy reminder.
am i destined to always undermine my mother?

ode to grief

oh wondrous sadness, please ruin me.
where else can i embody the quiver
of a cascading roar slicing right through me?

the anguish that hits in convulsions. how freeing
to be nothing but injury, nothing but crude lament
holding its breath and swallowing the unanswered pleas.

in the transient hush, i wait for relief that never breaks through,
i find comfort in misery, the blatant outpour of thought
that keeps me in oversaturated gloom.

please, how do i sculpt you a statue from the salt of my tears?
build you an altar from my spine? revere you as the blood
that courses within me. as if i'm only here to worship
the emptiness that's left behind.

crying together as catharsis

—for Maria, Eva, Rocio, and Cristina

at first, my sisters and i sit in a silence
only we understand—the dense halt before breaking.

in the cemetery, the grass is uniform
the sky is the right shade of blue
we search for meaning in everything
but the world is plain and we are still hollow.

at least, right now, we feel it together.
the dry pull of grief that is now a firm constant
in our lives. it has reshaped us
into daughters who cry under the endless sky.

in between tears, one of us suddenly says something
that makes us laugh. a memory held dearly
and only opened here where we can summon
our mother's presence with our exhale.

the air around us holds her suspended
between this realm and the next.
and we are the living embodiment of her echo.

the five of us congregate as if this mundane
patch of earth where she lays buried
is now our place of worship. we don't need to speak
about the ache, it exists simply as breathing.

those who hunger & thirst

the virgin mary cradles me through queerness

she holds me as i scream,
lets me curse god's name

like anger masking misery,
like i'm tired of blaming myself
for something i can't fix.

she watches as i renounce
the faith i've held onto,

as i sever my relationship with god
like i'm purposely rejecting
what previously was a vital organ.

i patch up the lacerations
with offbeat prayers,
with makeshift altars attempting to reclaim
my softness as a strength.

the virgin mary cloaks me with her mantle
encrusted with ancient nebulas.
within it, i rest the weariness of my bitter gloom.

all that's left of me is desolation
seeking comfort in the metaphysical
that hasn't abandoned me.

like a holy mother is what i need
to survive the loneliness.
like i can't talk to the mother i have in living flesh,
who is blinded by tradition.

the virgin mary lets me
empty myself each morning.

she sits with me in the silence
of my jaded disposition,
in my crude abandonment,
in my stubborn heartache.

half love | full love

the man loves me in silence,
parasocial dreaming that leaves him
staring at me from afar.

i'm a wish he doesn't commit to,
regret personified that always haunts,
a whisper that visits him in dreams.

he says his head is full of me.
i know, i feel it: i've reluctantly lived
in a purgatory made from his skin

like i'm fated to burn in his presence,
i feed the flame as if i'm made from it.
man who also burns and doesn't say it,

lets himself be ash,
leftover cinders that collapse
under the weight of his insincerity.

i let him love me here,
where i'm made of kerosene.
the endurance slowly kills me.

sacred anger

this is an exorcism. the rage
demands the hurt to pour out.

from me, everything i never released
comes out untamed and wild in raw exposure.

we sit in it, the fire that burns the remnants
of my dead carcass. what pity, to witness

the shriveled shape of who i used to be. let me have
this last frenzied cry, voice hoarse from years of screaming

at nothing but the dark. the loneliness i chewed on as sustenance.
please, help me tend to the kindling where my abandonment combusts.

the satisfying and relentless purging. i am ripe fruit
born from feral heartache. the seed that survived

in scorching flame and has sprouted
in the leftover smoke.

genesis after depression

at first, i was only dust
composed of blackened ash.

leftover disarray
claiming to be soil.

a lump of nothing
from which i molded a new body,

breathed soul into it
and named it: new self,

named it: eve reclaiming eden,
named it: adam was always a coward.

named it: complacent man
deserves no higher wisdom.

but me? i am god
created in my own image.

burning, 7:17 am

i awake from another dream he's in,
the center of my chest burning.

from within me, a glowing flood.
like movement that slowly goes inward.

i'm an oracle chasing a phantom.
i see him in the peripheral.

my head is full of relentless noise,
the inevitable wishes come to whisper.

unfolding, the visions i feel
but can't ever reach.

i'm an anxious song
sung in silence

about the yearning,
the failed attempt at forgetting.

the inkling, a cord pulsating
with light that draws me in.

a beacon that fills me with fire.

holy death | holy queer

disruptor of my life,
your blessed destruction.

the havoc you brought in your wake
broke me down into barren wilderness.
in the empty desert, i watched life pass me by.

i was bare bones clutching myself
through an arid wasteland where
disappointment spoke back to me.

holiness, i heard your whisper in the wind,
the alluring murmur wanted to find me
but i was fearful of stepping into the unexplored

landscape before me. the path illuminated by moonlight,
the darkness i had to nervously fumble through.
amid this loneliness, i learned to use my emotions as a guide.

within me, i unearthed and gave birth to a witch who invokes
catharsis, interprets shadows, walks through the night and feels.
knows the secrets that rise from the dead who speak

in nameless tongues. on this dry terrain, i cultivate survival.
i rest the weight of the oncoming journey solely on faith.
the desert welcomes me as its own.

pent up desire erupting at the first sign of safety

in small town texas, my legs pinned to a motel bed,
i was anxious body held by hungry hands.
us—nervous touch, careful fumbling,
skin beneath bare heat, the performance
of romantic feeling wrapped in calm trust.

i didn't know what it was like
to be wanted like this. flew halfway
across the country in search
of false comfort that didn't come.

for a week, my sense of self expanded
from this. i maneuvered undiscovered panic,
loved in the midst of precarious stability,
felt myself unfold in the grime of her unkempt
survival. we lived off 711 microwaveable meals,
weighted blanket, the four loko buzz.

my quiet whimpering sometimes quivered out
while she slept the depression away.
3 p.m. sitting next to her in the bed
that acted as our sanctuary in the cold weather.

i was only one person barely living.
only sad contemplation keeping
both of us scarcely fed with a small steady income.

as a pair, we were a cluster of desperate want,
sloppy misery crashing into each other.

but in the moment, that was love. the security
of being touched. the exhale of coming undone.
the collective feeling of surviving it together.

maladaptive daydream

disillusion, look at the mess.
past the obscure haze of empty promises,
the man is a myriad of leftover shit.

what do i do now that i'm discarded?
now that i'm no longer useful to him?

woe is me, look at the dysfunction
i enabled for years. how i let him dig in,
make barren home in my ribcage

and suck out the marrow. today, i'm anger
shaped like a knife defending my integrity.
today, i cut a hole in my chest,

i claw out the man who leeches.
and his face is carved like the imprint
of my father's dishonest greed.

cease to exist

—after Fiona Apple

if you stay, i'll let you suffocate me.
this is love, i think. the tension

boiling in the cramped space you keep me in.
does it matter that i can't breathe
if we're floating in the ether, surrounded by stars?

i'll wait for you, i'll exist only in the contained stories
we whisper to each other in the dark.
where no one else sees us, as the emptiness passes us by.

how does it feel to be a voyager trapped
in the heaviness with me? i've forgotten
what anything outside of this feels like,

have become accustomed to the disappointment
and mask it as prolonged patience. i'll silently burn here,
in the life i live through your gaze, the anxious performance

of eagerly amputating my limbs to fit into the meager
enclosure we float in. before us, i was
expansive light. what am i now but a small flame

struggling to stay alight in the limited oxygen?
what am i now but lover defined by how you watch me?
for you, i'll mold myself into something i don't recognize.

the poet refers to their past selves as “she”

in the old testament, god is a fat girl
grappling with elusive identity.

she is the giver of life,
who makes everything
out of nothing.

who uplifts revival as beauty.
wipes the earth clean. starts anew
with an untainted slate.

does this every time
there is too much destruction.

until all that’s left is forgiveness.
authenticity bare-skinned
reborn as a mortal vessel.

who sheds an old self,
claims a new identity,
and welcomes the gospel.

codependent love

my hands were makeshift rafts
and the weight of her body sat in them.

i wanted to be something more sturdy
than planks of emotion
fastened by tangled worry.

wished that i hadn't hastily carved myself out
from a thicket that was plagued
by woodboring creatures determined

to hollow me out
and force me to be their habitat.

as if i had the ability
to hold anyone else but myself.

when i became buoyant platform,
it was merely to stay afloat
in the waters of my despondency.

i was aimlessly adrift. at first,
there was only the unforgiving ocean

but then the convulsion of her shallow breath.
her quivering abandonment.

how i once had hoped to be given a lifeline.
so i offered myself as one.

returning

i can only describe it
as flooding. every repressed
feeling rushing through.

i hadn't realized
i was in love.

it happened somewhere
between pursuing him
and exchanging our truths.

the years coalesced
into a thread
of confusing emotions
that have bled into all that

i do. the way i tamed desire.
put a muzzle on my heart
and rebranded it as self-control.

how it came undone without trying.
my immediate unraveling
at the mention of pervasive danger.

the ingrained impulse
to shield him from it.
to be a place of safety.

i felt myself expand
as i collapsed. the realization
engulfing me and transforming me
into protective lover.

what else was i supposed to do
but come undone?

i welcomed the torrent, cried
as the floodgates opened,
handed myself over to feeling.

god only makes mistakes with intention

the archaeologist that digs up my body will tell you
the story of how i was carved out of eve's rib
one night in the desert after she was banished from eden.

after i die, the remnants of my carcass will reveal
that i'm ancient. i was alive for thousands of years.
that i was celestial soul trapped in human existence.

at the center of the carnal vessel that holds me, i'm
the replicated image of a creator made of pure light. i'm a six
winged seraph burning with the truth of an omnipotent god.

at my birth, the infinite sky accidentally filled me
and i became more astral than woman. what's gender
but purely a feeling? an extension of self,
a way of placing meaning on boundless experience.

inside me there is eternal sanctity, magnified purity
channeled through bloodstreams predestined to live
as an evolved ape. i was fated a life half-seen,
misinterpreted in the presence of generational curses.

i was born as consecrated essence incarnated
as human flesh. a child created in stardust molded
in the blurry fog of an outdated past. i'm uncovering
the authenticity found deep in my spirit.

i refuse to be perceived as anything less
than the multifaceted manifestation of the divine.

i create a dogma to worship myself with

if i don't, who will? who'll let me be religion?
bible written in the shape of a body? fat girl

who calls herself temple. who falls at her own feet
in penance and prays like she's her own living god.

says: body forgive me, i haven't done enough
to cherish the warmth of your sacred flesh. says:

let me come back hallowed, renewed, wholly
divine yet mortal being. celestial body. skin

that is pure human, that will someday die, won't
resurrect from a tomb after the third day. instead,

body that will rot, that has to give into impermanent
existence, the knowledge of a life that will someday end.

but does that mean i shouldn't praise this human flesh?
shouldn't protect it for surviving and striving to thrive

in conditions that others would've fled? does that
not make me a saint? or martyr? something close to god?

glorified fuckboy

lie to me. i'll believe in the intensity
of the damage between us, call it something
like spiritual love that tests me or the codependent
obsession i'd unthinkingly jump for.

how scary—to know i was ready
to give him my everything. how i got lost
in the sound of his voice worryingly
holding me on the other side of the phone.

why did he tell me? i could've stayed
another desperate bitch longing without
reciprocation. the desire built up
inside me without the false hope.

it would've been easier. i could've crashed
into the wall and then fallen apart on my own.
how dull, i thought if i stayed long enough,

he would finally see my whole worth.
call me a dumb bitch who wants love and receives
cathexis, the dysfunctional familiarity
that bled through the turbulent trauma bond.

maybe i shouldn't have waited around
like devoted stray pleading a man for kindness.
what was i supposed to do but believe his apologies?

we sat together in the heaviness, his arms
wrapped around me as i let out loud sobs.
the concerned tremble of reassurance
he spoke with, the regretful and quiet tone.

i would've done it. would've excavated
the old pain out of me, wiped the slate clean,
given him chance after chance.
i would've let the past go.

god is a twelve-year-old girl who has too many big dreams

at her altar, i give offerings
in the form of my chemical romance cd's
and the promise of a future worth living.

i've learned to worship her angsty word as creed.
the poems scribbled out while sitting in the middle of class.
the farfetched daydreams. the innocence unfolding
as scrupulous honesty she yet hasn't learned how to wield.

daily, i pray to her for protection
from all that has ever been imposed on me.
she gifts me virtuous truth and i let her mold
the person i'm continuously becoming. under her guidance,
she gifts me forgiveness for sins i've committed against her.

my god lets me come back, doesn't expect
anything but my trust. through me, i let her explore
new experiences with candor: i'm a vessel
preaching her gospel, devoted disciple giving
my heart in her honor. i'm a faithful believer.

within me, i build her a church made from
the scraps of everyone i've ever been.
together, we invoke litany that calls me
back into authenticity. with fervor, i vow
to never forget: i kneel and revere
my almighty god who lives timidly
in the awkwardness of tween sincerity.

like a good bitch

like a good bitch
i beg for the scraps from the table
i patiently wait to be fed

i treat the leftover scraps
as if they are a salivatory delicacy.

call me a good bitch
loyal retriever
flea bag full of hunger

who stays and sits on command.
who is trained to self-betray
in exchange for scarce reward.

like a good bitch
i'll be the guard dog
the protective defender

who barks at the oncoming danger.
who heels and prepares to attack.

god is nonbinary

god is genderless, with no face
and no limbs, a shapeless figure.

god is an omnipotent light
eternally emitting the universe.

god isn't anything
and yet is everything:

the sound of echoes fading,
the chill of late september,

the air of the room i cried in
for months, where i lost myself

and found myself again created
in the image of the almighty lord.

i met god in the flowy ether of intuition
that comes in the dead of night,

when i emptied myself of false beliefs
and became a barren slate asking to be filled.

god came down from heaven
and baptized me again in a new name,

called me: prophet who builds a queer kingdom,
witch who has been gifted the craft of healing

and enacts it in the name of the lord.
god said: go and spread my word,

replace the false prophets who spew lies
about my children, the downtrodden

who've been persecuted in my name,
do this and uplift the divinity of queer.

that is now your holy mission
given unto you by i, the lord.

the merciful & the persecuted

i decide to be god

for once, i will have songs
sung to me in penance.
whole choirs made of men
born from jaded tongues.

the prodigal sons who return
with their prayers. the men who
cast their stones. the men who drank
my blood. the men who burned themselves
alive and then placed the blame on me.

each is destined to come back.
they will step timidly into the chapel
made of crystal light. within me,
they will ask for unconditional benevolence.

with their hands outstretched
in reverence to clemency,
they will kneel in the echoing silence.

for once, i will get to bestow my judgment.
and they will wait in the suspended stillness
of their inevitable submission.

my father is a stranger i try to ignore

my father is a stranger i try to ignore
sits on half of my body.

he is hefty weight that anchors me
to a past where i wear the mask
of the person i failed to be.

in the mirror, he's etched on my face.
his unsteady facade of loneliness
disguised as unwavering arrogance.
his protective self-defense.

i've learned the art of mimicking
his disasters. decorate myself
with self-imposed isolation,

shaky pride. stubborn anxiety.
anything that feeds the narrative
of unfair disadvantage.

like him, i step carefully around
the land mines of my body.
become a waiting bomb
that accidentally detonates in front of him.

an anxiety attack of shaking arms
begging him to leave. from my mouth,
i unleash a lifetime of bottled up outrage
in the shriek of a trembling scream.

he doesn't know how to witness
the crude exposure of his failure.
can't hold me for who i am. doesn't see me.

i push back. his pride swells in him.
a silent eruption that builds in his chest
for two months. until my mother's death

breaks him down in guilt. between sobs,
he tries to apologize. an outburst
quivering through him.

i do what he couldn't: i quietly hold him
through the howling. his loud bawling
resonating against my swelled chest.

living on second street

after the late night cramming,
books half-read in the dim light,
there was the routine thud of the metal
coming in from the railyard.

every day, the same tired habits.
the mornings spent rushing out
of the small house without enough

room to breathe. the cockroaches
we lived with, the dogs that barked too much.
the way the noises bled into each other
as a restless cacophony.

all i had was a half room pressed against
the peeling paint. beige walls covered
in teenage dreams next to a broken bed.

my sister and the allegiant secrets we kept
tucked in the small room we shared.
a bubble of security within the sagging house
that gave in under the tension

of the father who yelled too much, the mother
who was always too tired. the sisters toppled
over each other trying to grasp tightly
onto the years between adolescence and adulthood.

home

—for Miguel

in the gray room
in the blue room
in the pink room,

we are laughter.
what sweetness,

this life where family
brings itself into existence.
decides to be more
than we were taught to be.

friend, we are destined
to love each other
like chosen blood,

like the rubble in your father's yard
could light aflame and we would still be safe
inside the walls we've created ourselves in.

sometimes, late at night,
surrounded by smoke under the dim lights
that illuminate the gray couch,
we whisper secrets

to one another about the lives
we'll someday live. here, i lose myself
and you fill me up again with dreams,

lighthearted peace. i'm new to loving
someone without the disaster. what beauty
you gift me. like trust was molded from our names

and we were once starstuff
coexisting through eternity
next to each other. what fantasy.

san bernardino, 2017

in april, when jonathan was killed
at the elementary school
across from my house,
the cops arrived

in a clan of rifles.

the eerie loudness bled in
through my bedroom window,
our driveway was a stage

for tv interviews
and strangers who crowded
the front yard.

everyone waited
in anticipation
to place the blame
on a single culprit.

a supposed isolated incident:
man loses control of the violence.

*

in june, there was a neo-nazi rally
on the other side of the city.

the mob swarmed the intersection
of the 2015 mass shooting location.

they used it as an excuse to spout
islamophobic lies fed through fragile channels.

it was a week after my mother's death,
i'd had enough of the loathing. used
the second stage of grief to yell
at the counterprotest.

the cops arrived in a clan of batons.

they circled us: state-sanctioned
threat protecting white supremacy.
they dictated the narrative.

decided who was dangerous.
decided who was not.

revolutionary rebirth

—for my comrades

through the months of suspended silence
that came after the destruction,
when i was relearning how to piece myself together,

i prayed to god asking for a love
with the capacity to hold me.

i was trying to summon true self
but they were merely a thought
trapped in the confinements
of a life i was outgrowing.

in the bleak dissociative fog,
i thought i was a defective fragment.
i swallowed the violence.

placed my value on production
even through grief, with the ache
pulling like an exposed abrasion.

there was always the questions,
about the *after*—once people
expected me to be something other

than grieving daughter. they asked
about money, a job, labor disguised
as questions concerned with my survival.

as if i wasn't exerting full effort
into still breathing under the weight
of depression that sat on my chest.

i dangled in pure feeling, couldn't sell
myself or my mourning. waited
for anything with a semblance to death

but, instead, was gifted a rebirth.
the respite in the form of community.
self forming through the ruins, i was held

with a tenderness that can only be given
through love as revolution. that doesn't
rely on productivity. that can make space
for personhood even through the rubble.

that doesn't ask about the *after*
or expect anyone to compartmentalize the flood.

where i was fully seen through the grief.
and the raw exposure of emotion i sat in
was welcomed and treated as power.

mourning the living

at the end, there was mostly the yelling.
pride stuck in between friendship rapidly falling apart.

the tension that dragged on for months,
i could feel the meticulous ripping.

the strain between us
was caked in sloppy sorrow.

the nights we dissolved into mush,
got high, and cried about men

who didn't properly love us. the secrets
we barely contained. the cycles

we said we would break from.
i had lost her once before,

the year she glued herself to him.
a codependence that bled

as dysfunctional relationship.
my best friend and our disconnection,

how she came back when he failed her.
i thought we'd learn to hold each other

again in a way that centered our tenderness.
that this time we would succeed in being

grounded protection in the midst of the flailing.
for a moment, i thought we'd achieve it.

on the horizon, there was boundless future,
a home full of wonder. something close

to family would be enough. could be
enough if it wasn't for the self-sabotage.

the retracted patterns. the way she minimized
the years she'd spend lamenting to me

about how he hurt her. how suddenly
the space where i had kept her safe

was weaponized and treated as trap.
and the fight where i tried not to lose her

again, where i pushed back. refused to enable.
was the yelling that drove us apart.

god asks me for penance about sodom and gomorrah

god kneels in front of me and sobs/ says he shouldn't
have enacted the carnage/ says he's plagued with guilt
that doesn't let him sleep/ says that everyone should've
been worthy of saving/ even with sin/ even with sodomy/
even with intimate cravings of flesh without the intention
to procreate/ god says the hatred that's been born in his image
wasn't worth the temporary discipline/ says he should've
let abraham bargain again/ says he should've spared the city
even if no one was righteous/ says he'll do better now/
says he won't justify genocide again/ even when it's done
in his name/ says he knows thousands have been killed
and burned at the stake for their queerness/ says he knows
it's his fault/ says he's sorry he can't bring them back
or resurrect them like jesus/ but that we will live eternally
in heaven/ that we will be reborn again/ this time
without the impact of the hatred that kills us/ this time
with the peace that is rightfully ours.

emptiness is totally vibe-able

the space that used to hold you
is an absence i'm learning to maneuver.

every day, i bargain with the god that controls the past,
i try to offer other friendships that hold less meaning.
that didn't cradle me through the rebirth.
a small conversation turns into something bigger.

how the depression threatened to swallow
but we were two a.m. confidants
spilling secrets through dimly lit screens.

a pair of dysfunctional endurance
getting through the humdrum.
our inner teens connecting
in an unstable adulthood.

you: sometimes drunk, pouring
tenderness to me through a chat box.
me: sometimes crying, asking you
for understanding through the ranting.

we held one another fifty miles apart.
sometimes acting like the only place
that would softly tell each other the truth.

but then the misdirected frustration.
the consequence of projection.
the pregnant silence that ended
in defeated argument.

about the responsibilities that weren't
mine to hold. about the insecurities
that had nothing to do with me.

you: flustered, fumbling. desperately trying
to salvage a relationship full of endless damage.
me: discarded, hurt. adamantly refusing
how you forced me to hold it.

i was born on this earth to save it

but i haven't decided if i'm
jesus or the virgin mary yet.
all i know is i'm holy.

someday, after my death,
i'll be able to grant miracles
for the worthy.

they won't have to pray or kneel
or coax me out with a promise
that they'll rectify their sins.

from heaven, i'll be patron saint
of outcasts, fems, queers, people
who exist constrained within lives

where they're forced to choose
between living visibly (in danger)
or going perpetually unseen.

together, all of us are destined to thrive eternally
in paradise. long after we've lived,
we'll have sacred books written of our stories:

the ancestral prophets we lost to the epidemic,
the gender alchemists who reclaim the craft
despite the persecution, the culture-shifting clerics
who deliver their sermons with trembling voices.

someday, we'll be uplifted and treated as sages,
mystics, creators of freedom and fluidity.

within us, we'll create a portal that brings
humanity closer to spirit and we'll ascend
to the gates of the heavenly kingdom

where we'll be welcomed
by marsha, leslie, sylvia.
the sound of our elders
singing us home.

meeting my father's mistress

the year after my mother's death,
my sister and i visited family in mexico.

the trip was an accidental pilgrimage.
we carried her memory with us
as we crawled through the foreign city streets
and every aunt or cousin who hugged us
was a living shrine to the ongoing grief.

my blood and my sister's blood were the only
two relics we had to offer everyone who asked
about her passing. who wanted to mourn her
together. who gifted us stories about her life
before either of us existed.

in mexico, we gave my mother another goodbye.
we laid her to rest in a tomb that existed
in the hearts of everyone who wept through the distance.

we were a procession of lost offspring
who were grappling with living without our matriarch.
her image followed us through our visit
but she was merely a spirit. a glimmer of the past
my father was desperately wanting to leave behind.

while my sister and i made ourselves messengers
who were bringing closure across the border,
my father was a vagabond who freely hopped
between countries. who equated cowardice
with freedom. who used my mother's death
as a way to bring his affair to light.

in the crowded room where we celebrated
my cousin's wedding, i watched my father's
mistress snake her way to us fixed to his hip.
the woman, a shadow of the life he lived without us,
was thin with a graceless presence.

in her gawky gauntness, she fit perfectly
beside him. they molded into each other
like two inept creatures sucking life out of nothing.

my sister and i shifted in our seats,
the uncomfortableness of their tone deaf approach
leaving us with a tasteless bitterness.

i could see my sister's grief surface
in the way she stiffened her body.
i could see my father's futile attempt at a connection
in the way he touched the woman softly.

in a moment that seemed suspended in harsh stillness,
i had to decide if i would greet the woman with kindness.
in my father's face, i saw all the ways he purposely kept
his distance from us. the fruitless pursuit of acceptance
that constantly seemed out of reach.

with a sharp inhale, i leaned in with a smile
as he introduced her. my hand touching her hand,
my cheek touching her cheek, my father's gaze fixed on me,
my sister's standoff greeting contrasted against my warm tone.

i kept a polite facade, felt the swelling in my chest
but didn't act on it. i treated the woman as if she wasn't
the living embodiment of my parents' failed marriage.

i gifted my father this act of tenderness.
a form of forced closure between us, a release
into his new life. a deliverance away from me.

queer ten commandments

i'm burning bush calling out with the voice of god.
through me, prophecies pour out in licks of fire
foretelling a self-fulfilled exodus that will lead me to freedom.

somewhere, i'm pilgrimage splitting the sea.
the journey homebound to uncharted territories.

i declare divine laws exalting new glory.
the ten commandments proclaim:

i. you shall find god in community, like kin
molded from the same trans(cendent) spirit.

ii. you shall give birth to true self,
again, in renewed holy image.

iii. you shall not self-betray
or abandon yourself using a counterfeit bluff.

iv. remember to rest, every day.
as compensation for creating yourself.

v. honor your ancestors. the butches, queens,
gender expansive queers who came before you,
who paved the way for your liberty.

vi. you shall pray for the ones
who've been killed.

vii. you shall not let their fear
of your expansive love
stop you from feeling it.

viii. you shall not be tokenized for your identity,
your labor, your clout, your truth watered down
for people who don't want to hear it.

ix. you shall lie if it'll help you stay safe,
if your survival depends on forceful deceit.

x. you shall let your pain turn to resentment,
virtuous envy about everything
they've stolen from us.

Acknowledgments

Acknowledgements

First and foremost, I would like to thank everyone who saw my artistry, took it seriously, nurtured it, and gave me the determination to believe in myself.

Thank you to my Mama in heaven, who saw my passion for writing and taught me the importance of prioritizing my craft. This book is for you, Mama. Te amo con toda alma.

Thank you to Querencia Press and Emily Perkovich for giving this collection of poems a home and guiding me through the process of publishing this book.

Thank you to Sarah Lainez, Alisa Slaughter, and Joy Manesiotis for being wonderful mentors to me as a young writer.

Thank you to Christian Flores for being my second pair of hands and eyes through the process of editing this collection of poems as I was preparing to submit it to publishers.

Thank you to Miguel Rivera and Miguel Canchola for emotionally holding me through the toughest transition I had to make in the artistic direction of this book.

Thank you to Bridget Miles for being there when I needed courage and for helping me conceptualize the outline of the book's structure that brought it to life.

Thank you to Gaby Cruz for being sunlight through the darkness and for always having faith in my vision.

Thank you to Gem Milsom for continuously supporting the evolution of my craft and for encouraging me to unapologetically dig into my artistic truth.

Thank you to my "Back Pain" group chat homies for accompanying me through the toughest of times, for helping me survive through the worst of it.

Thank you to my beautiful family and friends, who had to listen to me obsessively talk about this book over the past few years and who faithfully cheered me on. I couldn't have written this book without y'all. Thank you for gifting me with your knowledge, your presence, your support.

Lastly but most importantly, thank you to all coming-of-age queers, brown fems, catholic mystics, and grieving children out there. This book is for us.

Printed in the USA
CPSIA information can be obtained
at www.ICGtesting.com
CBHW050616081124
17080CB00040B/290

9 781959 118787